I0558455

"No amount of time can erase the memory of a
good cat, and no amount of masking tape can
ever totally remove his fur from your couch."

-Leo Deworken

A portion of sales will be donated to a local animal shelter.

Thank you to everyone who believed in my project and to those
who love Zeph almost as much as I do. Zeph wants to thank Fee
and Ozie for being understanding when he was the center of
attention during his photo shoots.

Special thanks to Analia Oliver (Instagram-@sixbunnyears)
for the beautiful illustrations that were so in line with my vision.

Books may be ordered at www.zigzagzeph.net
Instagram account-@zigzagzeph
To contact Meg or Zeph, email-zigzagzeph1@gmail.com

Library of Congress Control Number: 2022916038
ISBN-979-8-218-04724-5
Published by Meg Edson

Zig Zag Zeph Copyright © 2022 Meg Edson. All rights reserved.
This book or any portion thereof may not be reproduced or
used in any manner whatsoever without the express written
permission of the publisher except for the use of brief
quotations in a book review.

ZiG ZAG ZEPH

THE TRUE STORY
OF A SPECIAL CAT

Written by Meg Edson   Illustrated by Analia Oliver

Hi.

My name is Zepherus,
but my friends call me Zeph.
They also call me Zephfull,
Zephfree or Snotstick.

But let's stick with Zeph.

I have a disability or difference.
You can notice it right away
when I walk. I twist and turn
and can't walk in a straight line.

I am bowlegged and keep my tail
in a curl or flat across my back.
It helps me balance.

See, I was born with something
called Cerebellar Hypoplasia
(cer-e-bel-lar hy-po-pla-sia).
I know, it's a lot to pronounce.

So, from now on,
I'll just refer to it as CH.

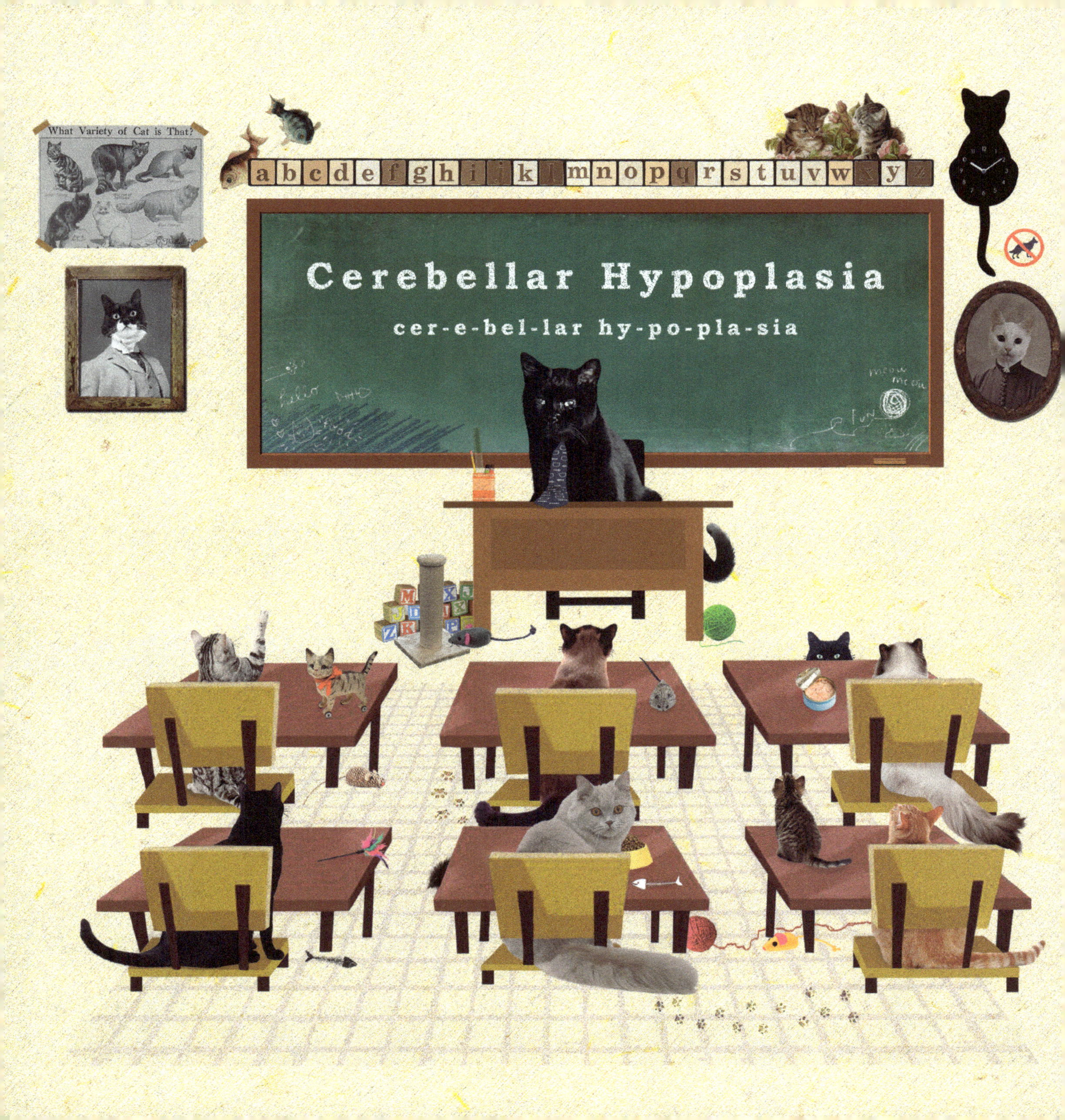

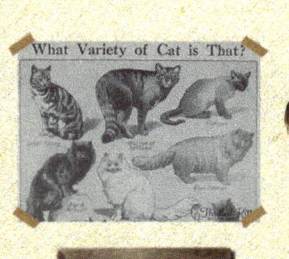

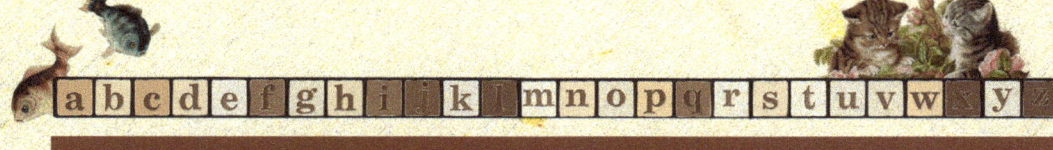

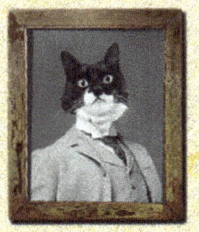

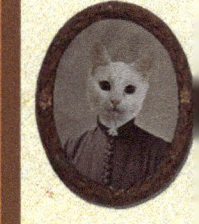

What Variety of Cat is That?
Cerebellar Hypoplasia
cer-e-bel-lar hy-po-pla-sia

When you have CH,

the part of your brain that helps with

balance doesn't develop right.

Some CH cats walk differently like I do,

but some can't walk at all.

But don't worry! They are carried

around, can still play and are happy!

My mom was sick when she had my sister
and me, so we both got it.

My sister's name is Feadora,
but I call her Fee.

Before I move on,

I must tell you something important.

Some people look at us and

think we are in pain.

We are not, as we don't know any better.

Fee and I think we are like any other cats.

Fee will walk a little, twirl around in a circle
and then fall on her side.

She needs to calm down and reset herself.

It's kind of like a time out.

She has a different brain like mine.

We don't meow.

Fee huffs.

HUFF HUFF

And I sound
like a turkey.

Warblegobblewarblegobblewarble

The good thing is that we eat and drink from dishes just like other cats.

But we are very messy! Because it is hard to keep from moving, we tend to drop our food into our water dish and on the floor.

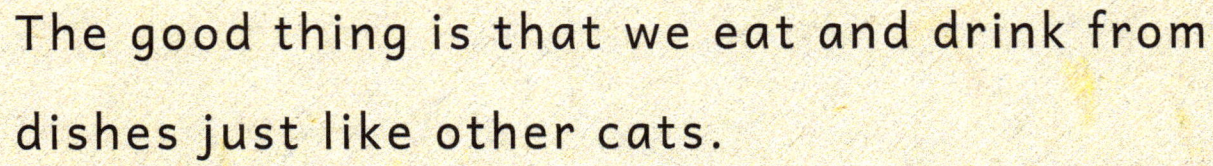

I have strong front legs
and can even climb a cat tree.
Having CH doesn't stop me

from doing anything.

Springs are my favorite toy.

I like to carry them around in my mouth

and play with them in the kitchen.

They go every which way just like me!

I love hanging out in the empty bathtub.

There are walls all around me

that I can lean on.

Sometimes I sneak a spring in there.

I have a permanent cold.

The doctors can't figure out what is going on.
I used to get drops in my nose and eyes,
but I hated it. It didn't help much since
I still sniffle, have runny eyes
and sneeze a lot.

I may go blind someday, but I will still find
my way around using my whiskers to guide me.

When I sneeze, a long piece of snot comes out. That's gross right? Sometimes it dries like that, which is why I am called Snotstick.

Along with my snotstick, sometimes water from my eyes dries near my nose and gets crusty.

I look funny and not so pretty.

But I say beauty is inside out
and that I am beautiful on the inside.
I am perfectly imperfect and filled with joy.

Well, I have talked a lot, especially for a cat.
Oops, I forgot to mention Ozilline!

She is not related, but I think of her like a sister.

Ozie does not have CH but only has one

ear, so I guess everyone has something.

Fee and I confuse her because sometimes
we bump into her but not on purpose.
She used to get upset and hiss.
Now she and I are best buddies.

It's time for a catnap.

Yes, it's true that cats take a lot of naps.

Writing a book

is exhausting!

But it was worth it because
I wanted to tell you about my life.

So if you get frustrated or have
trouble doing something,
don't give up!

Think of me, **Zig Zag Zeph,**
climbing to the top of my cat tree,
having fun and doing everything I want.

www.ingramcontent.com/pod-product-compliance
Lightning Source LLC
Chambersburg PA
CBHW051629140626
46547CB00033B/2940